D0948938

PARTY!

PARTY!

EASY RECIPES FOR FINGERFOOD AND PARTY DRINKS

Fran Warde   Photography by Debi Treloar

RYLAND
PETERS
& SMALL

LONDON NEW YORK

First published in the United States in 2003
by Ryland Peters & Small, Inc.
519 Broadway, 5th Floor
New York, NY 10012
www.rylandpeters.com

10 9 8 7 6 5 4 3

Printed and bound in China

Library of Congress Cataloging-in-Publication Data

Warde, Fran.
  Party! : easy recipes for fingerfood and party drinks /
Fran Warde ;
photography by Debi Treloar.
    p. cm.
Includes index.
  ISBN 1-84172-502-1
  1. Appetizers. 2. Cocktails. I. Title.
  TX740.W265 2003
  641.8'12--dc21
                                        2003005777

Commissioning Editor Elsa Petersen-Schepelern
Editor Sharon Ashman
Production Louise Bartrum
Art Director Gabriella Le Grazie
Publishing Director Alison Starling

Food Stylist Fran Warde
Stylists Emily Chalmers and Helen Trent
Indexer Hilary Bird

Notes
All spoon and cup measurements are level unless
specified otherwise.
Ovens should be preheated to the specified temperature.
If using a fan-assisted oven, cooking times should be
reduced according to the manufacturer's instructions.
Specialist Asian ingredients are available in larger
supermarkets and Asian stores.
Uncooked or partially cooked eggs should not be served
to the very young, the very old, people with compromised
immune systems, or to pregnant women.

Recipes in this book have previously been published in *Food
For Friends* and *Simply Delicious Food* by Fran Warde.

contents

party time

Everyone loves a party. As the host, you will want your friends to have lots of fun, but your guests will also want to see you enjoying yourself—while serving beautiful drinks and delicious food with the greatest of ease and style. This book will help you throw a party that is both enjoyable and memorable.

Food and friends go hand in hand, so if you are organizing a get-together, whatever the number of guests, you will want to serve some food. The style of party you choose to give will dictate the food you offer. So here you will find a great selection of ideas from quick, easy nibbles to serve at an impromptu gathering, to more substantial recipes for planned parties and special celebrations. There are also sweet treats—party style—and of course, great suggestions for chic cocktails that will get any party buzzing with excitement. All the recipes can be eaten standing up with nothing more than a napkin to catch the odd crumb. Even the sweet treats are small for easy handling.

The recipes in this book are simple to follow and designed not to take up too much of your precious party time. The best hosts are those who want to enjoy themselves rather than slaving in the kitchen while their guests are having all the fun. So get organized and prepare as much as possible in advance. Your friends have come to spend time with you and meet new people. If you are the best host in town, your guests will have great food and refreshments, a fun evening with you, and maybe even collect a new telephone number or two. Get planning, inviting, marketing, cooking, and then open your doors for a great party. Yes, it's that simple!

nibbles and dips

spiced nuts

Let the nuts cool before eating. They can be made the day before the party, just make sure you store them in an airtight container until needed.

1 teaspoon cumin seeds

1 teaspoon fennel seeds

1 teaspoon Spanish sweet smoked paprika

1 teaspoon sea salt flakes

2 tablespoons olive oil

⅓ cup cashews, about 3 oz.

⅓ cup brazil nuts, about 3 oz.

⅓ cup almonds, about 3 oz.

⅓ cup peanuts, about 3 oz.

⅓ cup shelled pistachios, about 3 oz.

2 baking trays

serves 4

Crush the cumin and fennel seeds coarsely with a mortar and pestle. Transfer to a bowl and add the paprika, salt, and oil. Mix well, then add all the nuts and mix again until the nuts are well coated.

Spread the nuts in an even layer on the 2 baking trays and roast in a preheated oven at 350°F for 10 minutes. Remove from the oven and turn the nuts with a spoon so they cook evenly. Return them to the oven and roast for a further 10 minutes. Remove from the oven, set aside to cool, then serve.

parmesan and rosemary wafers

These are a must for any good party. Everyone will be constantly nibbling, so make plenty. They can be made in advance but they must be kept chilled in an airtight container.

2 sprigs of rosemary, leaves stripped and finely chopped

8 oz. Parmesan cheese, coarsely grated, 3 cups

2 baking trays, lined with parchment paper

makes 24

Put the rosemary and Parmesan in a bowl and mix. Put teaspoons of the mixture in little heaps on the baking trays and flatten out into circles. Make sure they are not too close, because they will spread in the oven. Bake in a preheated oven at 400°F for 8–10 minutes, or until golden. Remove from the oven and let cool. Gently peel off the paper and serve.

crispy noodles

These rice vermicelli snacks are known as *mee krob* in their homeland of Thailand. They are always popular, so be sure to make plenty for your gathering. The vegetables can be chopped in advance but the vermicelli should be cooked at the last minute for a crispy, fresh flavor.

2 oz. rice vermicelli

1 onion, finely chopped

1 garlic clove, chopped

1 inch fresh ginger, peeled and chopped

1 fresh red chile, chopped

a bunch of cilantro, chopped

a bunch of chives, chopped

2 heads mini lettuce, such as romaine hearts

sunflower oil, for deep-frying and stir-frying

makes 20

Fill a wok one-third full of oil and heat. To test if the oil is hot enough to begin cooking, add a piece of vermicelli; it should puff up immediately. If it sinks to the bottom, heat the oil a little more.

Add the vermicelli in small handfuls, turning it with tongs to help it puff up evenly, this will take 40–60 seconds. Remove the vermicelli to a plate lined with crumpled paper towels. Pour the oil into a heatproof container.

Wipe out the wok and return to the heat. Add 1 tablespoon oil, then the onion, garlic, ginger, and chile. Stir-fry for 5 minutes.

Turn off the heat, add the cooked noodles to the wok, and mix well. Stir in the herbs.

Break the lettuce leaves away from the stem and wash and dry them. Fill them with spoonfuls of the noodle mixture, and arrange on a plate to serve.

artichoke hummus with ciabatta

You can make this dip the night before. Just remember to remove it from the refrigerator a while before serving so the flavors can warm up. Instead of ciabatta bread, you can serve the hummus with cheese straws, grissini (Italian breadsticks), pita, or other bread for dipping or spreading.

10 oz. artichoke hearts in olive oil, drained

4 oz. canned pinto beans or chickpeas, drained, about ½ cup

sea salt and freshly ground black pepper

to serve

ciabatta bread, toasted

cheese straws or grissini

serves 4

Put the artichoke hearts and beans in a food processor or blender and process until smooth. Transfer to a bowl and season with salt and pepper to taste. Serve the hummus with the toasted ciabatta and cheese straws or grissini.

raw vegetable platter

A selection of fresh vegetables makes a stunning centerpiece.

8 carrots, cut into batons

8 baby fennel bulbs, trimmed and halved

1 cucumber, cut into batons

2 bunches of radishes, trimmed

½ cup extra virgin olive oil

3 tablespoons balsamic vinegar

serves 12

Arrange the raw vegetables on a big serving plate. Put the oil and vinegar in a small dipping bowl and mix. Serve with the vegetables.

potato skins with green dip

The cheese can be either melted and soft or crisp and crunchy—keep checking and remove from the oven at the right moment. Save the potato middles for another day.

12 large baking potatoes

¾ cup olive oil

16 oz. sharp Cheddar cheese, grated, about 4 cups

green dip

1¾ cups sour cream

2 bunches of chives, chopped

2 bunches of scallions, chopped

a bunch of flat-leaf parsley, chopped

sea salt and freshly ground black pepper

a baking tray, lightly oiled

serves 24

Using a small, sharp knife, pierce each potato right through the middle. Bake in a preheated oven at 350°F for 1 hour 10 minutes, or until cooked through. Remove and set aside until cool enough to handle. Cut each potato in half lengthwise, and scoop out the soft potato middles with a spoon, leaving a thin layer lining the skin. Cut each skin half into 4 wedges, then cover and refrigerate until needed. (You can prepare the potatoes ahead to this point the day before the party.)

To make the dip, put the sour cream, chives, scallions, and parsley in a bowl. Add salt and pepper to taste and mix well.

Brush oil over the potato skins and arrange in a single layer on the baking tray. Bake on the top rack of a preheated oven at 425°F for 30 minutes, or until golden, moving the potato skins around occasionally so they cook evenly. Remove from the oven and reduce the heat to 400°F.

Sprinkle the potato skins with cheese and return to the oven for 5–10 minutes, until the cheese is melted or crunchy, checking after 5 minutes if you want it just melted. Serve with the green dip.

bread, wraps, and rolls

sage and stilton flatbread

Serve this with drinks when your guests arrive. If Stilton is not your favorite cheese, try using another blue cheese such as Roquefort or Gorgonzola, or try Brie or a hard cheese, such as a mature Cheddar.

3⅓ cups all-purpose flour

1 teaspoon baking powder

1 cup plain yogurt

1 stick butter, melted

2 eggs, beaten

3 tablespoons chopped fresh sage

4 oz. Stilton cheese, crumbled, 1 cup

a baking tray, lightly oiled

serves 8

Sift the flour and baking powder into a bowl and make a well in the middle. Put the yogurt, melted butter, eggs, and sage in a separate bowl and mix. Pour the yogurt mixture into the well in the flour and stir with a wooden spoon until well blended.

Knead the dough into a ball, put on the oiled baking tray, and roll it out to a circle about 12 inches diameter. Cook in a preheated oven at 350°F for 20 minutes. Remove the bread from the oven, crumble the Stilton over the top, and return to the oven for a further 10 minutes. Remove the bread from the oven and let cool a little. Transfer to a large chopping board, cut into wedges, and serve.

grissini sticks with prosciutto

It's best to shop for these ingredients at an Italian gourmet store, as the grissini will be skinny and crunchy, made with good flour in the traditional way, and the prosciutto can be sliced to order. Assemble these up to an hour in advance of your party.

12 very thin slices prosciutto

12 grissini

serves 12

Trim off the excess fat from the prosciutto and wrap a slice around the top half of each grissini. Arrange in glasses or on a large plate and serve.

garlic and parsley bread

Everyone loves this easy bread, which makes ideal party food. It's at its best if you broil it at the last minute then serve it immediately, while still warm.

3–4 garlic cloves, finely chopped

a bunch of flat-leaf parsley, chopped

½ teaspoon hot red pepper flakes

2 loaves ciabatta bread, split lengthwise

olive oil, for sprinkling

sea salt and freshly ground black pepper

serves 8

Spread the garlic, parsley, pepper flakes, salt, and pepper evenly over the opened bread halves. Sprinkle generously with olive oil, then cook under a preheated broiler until golden. Cut the bread into chunks and serve at once.

rice paper packages with dipping sauce

These are time-consuming but worth it, so enlist some help before the party to assemble them. They can be made up to 4 hours in advance, but they must be covered with a damp cloth and plastic wrap, then chilled until needed.

12 rice paper wrappers*

2 carrots, cut into matchsticks

6 scallions, cut into matchsticks

4 oz. bean sprouts, about 1 cup, rinsed and trimmed

leaves from a bunch of Thai basil

a bunch of watercress

1 tablespoon toasted sesame seeds

dipping sauce

2 tablespoons honey

1 tablespoon soy sauce

1 tablespoon teriyaki sauce

1 red chile, thinly sliced

serves 12

Soak the rice paper wrappers in several changes of warm water until soft, about 4 minutes.

Gather up little clusters of the carrots, scallions, bean sprouts, basil, and watercress and put a cluster in the middle of each of the softened wrappers. Sprinkle with sesame seeds and roll up to enclose the vegetables.

To make the dipping sauce, put the honey, soy sauce, and teriyaki sauce in a small bowl and mix. Add the chile and transfer to a small, shallow dish to serve with the packages.

*Note Vietnamese dried rice paper wrappers (bánh tráng) are sold in Asian markets in quantities of 50–100. The packages can be resealed and kept in a cool pantry.

vegetarian mexican rolls

These are best made to order or at the last moment, otherwise the avocado will discolor. You could encourage everyone to roll their own by setting out all the fillings in bowls and leaving the avocados whole, for everyone to slice as needed.

12 soft large flour tortillas

8 oz. cream cheese, 1 cup

4 carrots, grated

a bunch of cilantro, chopped

a bunch of chives, chopped

a bunch of scallions, chopped

2 chiles, chopped

4 avocados, halved, pitted, peeled, and sliced

freshly squeezed juice of 2 lemons

¼ cup olive oil

sea salt and freshly ground black pepper

serves 24

Put each tortilla on an individual sheet of plastic wrap. Spread with the cream cheese and then sprinkle evenly with the carrot, cilantro, chives, scallions, and chiles. Flatten the topping lightly with a spatula.

Put the avocado slices in a bowl and sprinkle with lemon juice, oil, salt, and pepper. Arrange over the open tortillas. Roll each tortilla into a tight cylinder, using the plastic wrap to help you roll. Twist both ends in opposite directions to make a cigar shape. Chill until needed, then slice in half, with the plastic wrap still on, and serve.

chicken salad wraps

Chicken is always a popular ingredient, and these wraps will satisfy your hungry guests. They can be made up to 4 hours in advance and chilled until needed. If you prefer to make these into bite-size offerings, slice each cylinder diagonally into about eight pieces just before serving, then pierce them with a toothpick for easy handling.

12 soft large flour tortillas, preferably whole-wheat

¾ cup mayonnaise

6 teaspoons whole-grain mustard

6 cooked chicken breasts, shredded

6 carrots, grated

¼ white cabbage, thinly sliced

6 medium tomatoes, thinly sliced

sea salt and freshly ground black pepper

serves 12

Lay each tortilla flat on a piece of waxed paper. Spread with the mayonnaise and mustard.

Sprinkle with the shredded chicken, grated carrot, sliced cabbage, salt, pepper, and tomato.

Roll up the tortillas into tight cylinders, using the waxed paper to help you. Twist the ends of the paper to secure.

To serve, cut the cylinders in half diagonally.

mexican shrimp wraps

2 flour tortillas, 8 inches diameter

salsa

1 jalapeño chile, seeded and finely chopped

½ red onion, finely chopped

1 garlic clove, finely chopped

2 tomatoes, peeled, seeded, and chopped

3 tablespoons sour cream

sea salt and freshly ground black pepper

filling

½ avocado, peeled and sliced

freshly squeezed juice of ½ lime

3 oz. shrimp, cooked and peeled

a small bunch of arugula, about 2 oz., washed and dried

serves 20

These canapés are visually stunning. The shrimp can be replaced with chicken, cooked beef, or grated fresh vegetables such as carrots and radishes. A long, cool Mojito (page 58) is the perfect accompaniment to these wraps.

To make the salsa, put all the ingredients in a bowl and stir well.

Heat the tortillas in a dry skillet, then transfer to a large chopping board. Divide the salsa between them and spread out evenly. Top with avocado slices and a little lime juice, then add the shrimp and arugula.

Roll up tightly and wrap in plastic, twisting the ends to secure. Chill for 30 minutes, then slice each roll into 10 pieces and arrange on a platter to serve.

goat cheese and pepper crostini

You can bake the breadstick and assemble the crostini up to 1 hour in advance. Cover with plastic wrap and chill until needed.

1 thin French breadstick (*ficelle*)

6 oz. creamy fresh goat cheese, about ¾ cup

4 roasted red bell peppers, peeled

20 spears asparagus, cooked and refreshed in cold water

olive oil, for brushing

sea salt and freshly ground black pepper

a baking tray

serves 20

To make the crostini, slice the breadstick diagonally into 20 thin slices. Put the slices on the baking tray and brush with olive oil, then sprinkle with salt and pepper. Cook in a preheated oven at 375°F for 5 minutes, or until golden.

Arrange the crostini on a plate and spread with goat cheese. Cut the roasted peppers into thin strips. Put a pepper strip and a spear of asparagus on each crostini. Serve.

ciabatta pizzas

Other breads can be used in these fantastic, fresh-tasting pizzas, so don't go looking specially for ciabatta.

3 loaves ciabatta, sliced

3 garlic cloves, halved

about ¾ cup olive oil

12 ripe tomatoes, peeled and sliced

a handful of pitted olives

a bunch of marjoram

2 lb. fresh mozzarella cheese, drained and sliced

a bunch of basil

sea salt and freshly ground black pepper

a baking tray

serves 12

Broil the ciabatta slices under a hot broiler until lightly toasted, then rub with the cut side of the garlic. Put the garlic ciabatta on a baking tray and sprinkle with a little olive oil.

Arrange the sliced tomatoes on the bread, then add the olives, marjoram, mozzarella, basil, salt, and pepper. Sprinkle some more oil over the top.

Cook in a preheated oven at 350°F for 15–20 minutes, or until the mozzarella has melted. Remove from the oven, let cool, and serve.

light bites

artichoke and tomato pastry boats

1 cup all-purpose flour

a pinch of salt

2½ tablespoons vegetable shortening or lard, chilled and diced

3 tablespoons unsalted butter, chilled and diced

1–2 tablespoons ice water

4 baby artichoke hearts in olive oil, drained and cut into quarters

2 oz. buffalo mozzarella, drained and cut into 16 pieces

8 cherry tomatoes, halved

2 scallions, each cut into 8 pieces

1 egg yolk, lightly beaten

sea salt and freshly ground black pepper

2 baking trays, buttered

makes 16

These delicious little bites are easy to make but can be time-consuming to put together, so enlist some help. They can be made up to 2 hours in advance.

To make the pastry dough, sift the four and salt together into a bowl. Using your fingertips, rub in the shortening and butter until the mixture resembles bread crumbs. Add the water, mixing lightly with a knife to bring the dough together. Knead lightly on a floured work surface, then shape into a flattened ball, wrap in plastic wrap, and chill for at least 30 minutes.

Put the pastry dough on a lightly floured surface and roll out to a large rectangle. Using a sharp knife, cut the dough into 16 pieces, each measuring about 1½ inches square. Transfer to the baking trays.

Put a piece of artichoke, a piece of mozzarella, a tomato half, and a piece of scallion on top of each dough square, pushing them in lightly to secure. Brush the edges of the dough with egg yolk, then gently squeeze the edges together to form a boat shape. Season with salt and pepper.

Bake in a preheated oven at 350°F for about 12 minutes, or until golden and cooked. Serve warm or at room temperature.

smoked oyster and goat cheese pastries

I love smoked oysters and I don't think that enough people know about them, so make these little pastries and let everyone enjoy. They can be made up to 4 hours in advance.

1 sheet ready-made puff pastry dough

4 oz. soft, rindless fresh goat cheese, crumbled

6 oz. canned smoked oysters

1 egg, beaten

sea salt and freshly ground black pepper

a baking tray, buttered

serves 12

Cut the rectangle of dough in half lengthwise.

Put half the crumbled goat cheese down the middle of one piece of dough. Arrange half the oysters in a row on top of the goat cheese. Brush the beaten egg along both the long sides, fold the dough over lengthwise, and gently press the edges together to seal. Repeat with the other piece of dough and remaining cheese and oysters.

Lightly brush both puff pastry packages with beaten egg, then sprinkle with salt and pepper. Cut both packages into 1-inch slices, then transfer to the baking tray. Cook in a preheated oven at 400°F for 12 minutes, or until puffed and golden. Let cool to room temperature before serving.

tomato and goat cheese tart

Oh, how I love this tart—the crumbly, flaky texture of the puff pastry, the thinly sliced onions and roasted tomatoes, then melted goat cheese binding them all together. Puff pastry can be bought frozen or refrigerated. It even comes prerolled for the super-busy person. These tarts can be made up to 6 hours in advance, then just warmed in the oven at 300°F for 10 minutes if wanted hot.

2 sheets ready-made puff pastry dough

2 onions, thinly sliced

8 oz. baby tomatoes, roasted

6 oz. soft, rindless fresh goat cheese, crumbled

2 tablespoons olive oil

1 teaspoon sugar

sea salt and freshly ground black pepper

a saucer, 6 inches diameter

a baking tray, lightly oiled

serves 4

Cut out 2 circles from each sheet of dough using the saucer as a template. Transfer the circles to the baking tray, then prick the dough all over with a fork.

Bake the circles in a preheated oven at 375°F for 15 minutes, then remove from the oven.

Put the sliced onion in a bowl with the roasted tomatoes, goat cheese, olive oil, sugar, salt, and pepper and mix well. Divide the mixture among the tart crusts, spreading it evenly over the top and pushing down gently.

Return the 4 tarts to the oven and cook for 20 minutes, then reduce the oven temperature to 350°F and cook for a further 15–20 minutes, or until the tarts are lightly browned. Serve hot or at room temperature.

chinese duck forks

These duck morsels are sweet and delicious, and they look wonderful. Serve them skewered on little forks, or on some porcelain Chinese spoons.

1 duck breast, skinned

3 scallions, cut into 2-inch pieces, then thinly sliced lengthwise

4 inches cucumber, peeled, seeded, cut into 2-inch pieces, then thinly sliced lengthwise

chinese marinade

2 tablespoons soy sauce

2 tablespoons dry sherry

1 tablespoon sugar

2 whole star anise

2 inches fresh ginger, peeled and chopped

¼ cup plum sauce

12 small forks or porcelain Chinese spoons

serves 12

Put all the marinade ingredients in a small nonstick saucepan and heat to simmering point. Add the duck breast and simmer very gently for 6 minutes on each side. Remove the pan from the heat, cover, and let cool. When cool, slice the duck very thinly crosswise. Reserve the marinade.

Spread out the sliced duck breast, put a few scallions and cucumber strips at one end of each slice, and roll up tightly into packages. Push onto the forks or put in the Chinese spoons. Sprinkle with a little of the reserved marinade and serve.

figs stuffed with prosciutto

Fresh figs are irresistible, especially when they are paired with prosciutto. This is such a simple recipe, but I can assure you that your guests will love it.

16 ripe figs

16 slices prosciutto

makes 16

Stand the figs upright and, using a sharp knife, cut a cross in the top. Put a folded slice of prosciutto inside each one. Put the stuffed figs on a serving platter and serve immediately.

Alternatively, make these in advance of your party, cover them with plastic wrap and store in the refrigerator. Remove them 1 hour before serving.

chicken skewers
with sweet chile

Chicken skewers are always very popular, so it's worth making extra. You can use boneless chicken thighs, but always remove any excess fat (they may also need to cook for a little longer, as the meat is denser). These skewers can be made the day before the party, just cover them with plastic wrap and chill until needed. If you want to serve them hot, put them on a baking tray and cook at 350°F for about 12 minutes before serving.

12 boneless, skinless chicken breasts

2 tablespoons honey

1¾ cups chile sauce

olive oil, for brushing

24 bamboo satay skewers, soaked in water for about 30 minutes

serves 24

Cut each chicken breast into 10 cubes. Put the chicken cubes in a bowl, add the honey and chile sauce, and mix well. Cover and chill overnight. When ready to cook, thread the chicken cubes onto the soaked satay skewers. Heat the broiler to medium-high, then brush the rack of the broiler pan with oil. (Alternatively, cook the skewers on a grill.)

Add the chicken skewers to the rack and cook, in batches if necessary, turning frequently, for 25 minutes, or until the chicken is cooked through. Repeat until all the chicken skewers are cooked, then serve hot or cold.

honeyed chicken wings

These really should be called Last Lick Chicken Wings—anyone who eats them removes every morsel of flavor and sticky meat from the bones. Just watch out that they don't burn in the oven. They can be made 1 day in advance, just cover them with plastic wrap and chill until needed.

16 chicken wings

1 cup honey

1 cup chile sauce

sea salt and freshly ground black pepper

a bunch of radishes, trimmed, to serve (optional)

serves 8

Put the chicken wings in an oiled roasting pan. Cook them in a preheated oven at 400°F for 40 minutes, turning them after 20 minutes so they brown evenly.

Meanwhile, put the honey and chile sauce in a small saucepan. Season with salt and pepper to taste and bring to a boil. Pour the sauce over the chicken wings, mix well, and let cool. Serve with radishes, if using.

sweet treats

plum pastries

You don't have to restrict yourself to using plums and almonds for these easy pastries, you can fill them with any of your favourite fruit and nuts. They can be made up to 6 hours in advance.

2 sheets ready-made puff pastry dough

12 plums, halved and pitted

8 teaspoons honey

2 tablespoons slivered almonds

2 baking trays, oiled

makes 12

Cut each sheet of dough in half lengthwise to give 4 pieces of dough. Cut each piece of dough crosswise to make 3 rectangles each, there should be 12 in total.

Put 2 plum halves on each piece of dough, then sprinkle with the honey and almonds.

Bake in a preheated oven at 350°F for about 15 minutes, or until puffed and golden. Remove from the oven and serve hot or cold.

tiramisù

Foolproof and very quick to prepare, tiramisù is a wonderful dessert to serve a large group of people—it can be made in advance, doesn't need cooking or heating, and tastes so delicious that it is universally welcomed. I like to make it with amaretti cookies and present it in groovy glasses instead of one large serving bowl.

50 amaretti cookies, crushed

¾ cup Kahlúa (coffee liqueur)

⅓ cup brandy

½ cup strong black coffee

2 lb. mascarpone cheese, 4 cups

8 eggs, separated

½ cup sugar

8 oz. bittersweet chocolate, grated, or ¼ cup unsweetened cocoa powder

20 glasses or a 12-inch square serving dish

serves 20

Arrange a quarter of the crushed amaretti cookies at the bottom of the glasses or serving dish. Put the Kahlúa in a small bowl with the brandy and coffee and stir. Pour a quarter of this mixture over the crushed cookies in the glasses or serving dish.

Put the mascarpone, egg yolks, and sugar in a bowl and beat until smooth. Put the egg whites in a separate bowl and beat until stiff. Gently fold the egg whites into the mascarpone mixture.

Spoon a quarter of the mascarpone mixture over the cookies. Repeat the layers 3 times, finishing with a layer of mascarpone mixture.

Sprinkle the grated chocolate or cocoa over the top of the tiramisù and refrigerate overnight. Serve chilled or at room temperature.

Top tip: Instead of topping the tiramisù with grated chocolate, melt the chocolate in the microwave in a plastic bag tied securely to close. Make a small hole in one corner and pipe 20 squiggles onto waxed paper. Let set, then insert the chocolate shapes upright into the individual glasses.

raspberries in champagne gelatin

This simple but delicious combination is a refreshingly light way to round off an evening's indulgence. If champagne seems a bit decadent, use a good bottle of cava or an American sparkling wine. These gelled desserts can be made the day before and chilled until needed.

2 envelopes powdered gelatin, ½ oz. each, or 2 tablespoons

1 lb. raspberries, about 3 cups

1 bottle champagne, at room temperature

8 glasses

serves 8

Put 3 tablespoons hot water in a small bowl and sprinkle the gelatin over the top. Set aside in a warm place to dissolve, about 10 minutes.

Divide the raspberries among the glasses. Open the champagne and add a little to the dissolved gelatin. Transfer the gelatin mixture to a pitcher and add the remaining champagne. Mix gently so that you don't build up a froth. Pour into the glasses on top of the raspberries, then chill for 2 hours, or until set.

espresso granita

A refreshing end to a meal at a summer party. Good biscotti can be purchased ready-made from Italian and other gourmet stores. This can be made the day before and stored in the freezer until needed.

6 tablespoons sugar

9 tablespoons freshly ground coffee

to serve

biscotti

light cream (optional)

12 small glasses or espresso cups

serves 12

Put 12 small glasses or espresso cups in the freezer to chill. Put the sugar and coffee in a French coffee press. Add 3¾ cups boiling water and let stand for 5 minutes to develop the flavor. Plunge the press, pour the coffee into a heatproof pitcher, and let cool to room temperature before chilling in the refrigerator.

When very cold, pour the coffee into a bowl and freeze for 20 minutes, or until ice crystals have formed around the edge. Crush the crystals with a fork and return to the freezer. Repeat this process about 3 times until you have an even mixture of fine ice crystals.

Cover and return to the freezer until ready to serve. Serve the granita in the glasses or cups with a biscotti and a sprinkling of cream for anyone who prefers their coffee white.

mini chocolate brownie squares

Everyone loves brownies—rich, sticky, and chocolaty, they make the perfect party treat. These are at their best if made on the day of the party, but if you are busy make them the day before and store them in an airtight container until needed.

4 oz. good-quality bittersweet chocolate

1 stick unsalted butter

2 eggs, beaten

1 cup plus 2 tablespoons sugar

⅔ cup self-rising flour

⅛ cup pecans, chopped (optional)

a rectangular cake pan, 11 x 7 inches, lined with waxed paper

makes about 54

Put the chocolate and butter in a large saucepan and melt over low heat. Remove from the heat, add the eggs, sugar, flour, and pecans, if using, and mix well. Pour into the prepared cake pan, smooth over the surface and bake in a preheated oven at 350°F for 30 minutes.

Remove from the oven and let cool in the pan. When cool, take hold of the waxed paper and lift the slab of brownies out of the pan, then cut into bite-size squares.

Top tip: If there are any brownies left at the end of the party, they will keep for several days in an airtight container.

exotic fruit salad

Not an apple or orange in sight in this exotic fruit salad. I like it to be full of fruit from the tropics, chosen according to cost and what's in season. Include no more than four varieties, so the individual flavors will be strong and sharp.

fresh fruit, such as sweet pineapple, mango, papaya, bananas, lychee, watermelon, coconut, pomegranate, melon, passionfruit, or persimmon

freshly squeezed juice of 4 limes

serves 8

Prepare the chosen fruits, arrange on a serving dish, then squeeze the lime juice over the top. Serve with toothpicks or teaspoons, depending on the selection of fruit.

chocolate-dipped strawberries

Chocolate always makes a sensational dessert, but here I have balanced the chocolate with fruit, in this case strawberries. Any variety of fruit can be dipped. These can be made up to 2 hours in advance.

4 oz. bittersweet chocolate

4 oz. white chocolate

12 large strawberries

parchment paper
12 bamboo skewers

serves 12

Put the dark chocolate and white chocolate in 2 separate bowls and set the bowls over 2 saucepans of simmering water. When melted, dip the pointed end of each strawberry into one of the chocolates and transfer to a sheet of parchment paper. When the chocolate is set, slide each strawberry onto a skewer and serve.

party drinks

vodka cranberry floaters

This tastes and looks heavenly. The blueberries add a colorful touch to this vodka classic.

¼ cup vodka, chilled

½ cup cranberry juice

ice cubes, to serve

blueberries, to decorate (optional)

makes 1

Put the vodka in a tall glass and add the cranberry juice. Mix well. Add a few blueberries, then some ice cubes. Serve immediately.

pimm's cocktail

Use your own selection of fresh fruit, but orange, cucumber, and mint are traditional.

¼ cup Pimm's No. 1

1 cup lemonade

1 slice orange

2 sprigs of mint

2 slices cucumber

ice cubes, to serve

makes 1

Fill a highball glass with ice and add each of the ingredients in turn. Serve cold.

white wine fizz

1 bottle white wine, 750 ml
1 quart sparkling water
1 apple, sliced
1 lemon, sliced
1 orange, sliced
1 kiwifruit, sliced
ice cubes

serves 8

Put all the ingredients in a pitcher, mix, and serve.

brown cow

½ bottle Kahlúa, 350 ml
1 quart milk
ice cubes

serves 8

Put the Kahlúa, milk, and ice cubes in a pitcher and mix. Alternatively, put the Kahlúa in individual glasses, and top with milk and ice.

cosmopolitan

ice cubes, for shaking

2 tablespoons Absolut Citron vodka

2 tablespoons Cointreau

¼ cup cranberry juice

2 tablespoons freshly squeezed lime juice

a cocktail shaker

serves 8

Fill the shaker with ice cubes. Add the alcohol and juices and shake until well blended and chilled. Strain into cocktail glasses and serve.

sea breeze

¼ cup vodka

½ cup cranberry juice

¼ cup grapefruit juice

ice cubes, to serve

makes 1

Fill a highball glass with ice, add the vodka and then the fruit juices. Stir and serve.

french 75

2 tablespoons gin

2 tablespoons freshly squeezed lemon juice

a dash of sugar syrup

ice cubes, for shaking

6 tablespoons chilled champagne, ⅓ cup, plus extra to serve

a cocktail shaker

makes 1

Put the gin, lemon juice, and sugar syrup in the cocktail shaker. Add the ice cubes and shake.

Pour into a champagne flute, add the champagne, and top up with more champagne just before serving.

mojito

This is a fabulously refreshing drink. If you want to make it for more people, simply multiply the ingredients accordingly.

1 lime, cut into 16 pieces

enough mint tips to fill the glass halfway

2 teaspoons sugar

crushed ice

¼ cup dark rum

club soda, to taste (optional)

makes 1

Put the lime and mint in an old-fashioned glass, then sprinkle with sugar. Using a pestle or the back of a spoon, crush the lime, mint, and sugar until the sugar has dissolved.

Fill the glass with crushed ice, add the rum, and stir briefly. Add soda water to taste, if using.

lobby dazzler

For authenticity, you should really use kumquats in this recipe. If you have difficulty finding them, use satsuma or clementine segments instead.

3–4 kumquats, quartered

2 teaspoons sugar

crushed ice

¼ cup Absolut Kurant vodka or plain vodka

makes 1

Put the kumquats in an old-fashioned glass and sprinkle with sugar. Using the back of a spoon or a pestle, crush the kumquats and sugar until the sugar completely dissolves and all the fruit juice is released.

Fill the glass with crushed ice, add the vodka and stir briefly before serving.

bloody mary

If you want to provide some of your guests with a nonalcoholic version of this drink, you could make two pitchers—one with everything and the other without the vodka.

5 lemons

1 cup vodka

3 inches white horseradish, freshly grated, or 1 tablespoon bottled horseradish

1 tablespoon Worcestershire sauce

1 teaspoon Tabasco sauce

3 cups tomato juice, well chilled

freshly ground black pepper

to serve

celery stalks, with leaves

crushed ice

serves 4

Fill a large pitcher halfway with crushed ice. Cut 1 lemon into slices and squeeze the juice from the others. Add the lemon juice and slices to the pitcher, together with all the other ingredients except the celery. Mix well. Serve in highball glasses with a celery stalk.

mulled wine

Warm your house and make your guests' hearts glow with this beautiful spicy drink known as *glühwein*. If you're making it for a big party, add more wine and sugar to the pan as the evening wears on.

2 bottles red wine, 750 ml each

8 whole cloves

2 oranges

3 tablespoons brown sugar

2 inches fresh ginger, peeled and chopped

1 cinnamon stick

½ teaspoon freshly grated nutmeg

serves 4

Pour the red wine into a medium saucepan. Push the cloves into the oranges, then cut each orange into quarters. Add to the pan, together with the sugar, ginger, cinnamon, and nutmeg.

Heat the mixture to simmering point and simmer for about 10 minutes, then serve hot.

apple and mint fizz

There is something satisfyingly traditional about making your own drinks. This one is simple, refreshing, and very popular on hot summer days.

a large bunch of mint

2 quarts apple juice

1 quart sparkling water

ice cubes, to serve

makes about 3 quarts

Reserve some of the mint leaves for serving and put the remainder in a heat-proof pitcher. Add 1¼ cups boiling water, let cool, then chill.

Transfer to a large container and add the apple juice, sparkling water, and ice cubes. Chop the reserved mint leaves, sprinkle over the top, and serve.

ginger beer

This seems a large quantity of ginger beer but it's so easy to make and it does store well. Take care that the bottle tops are secure, as they can sometimes pop off.

3 unwaxed lemons

3¼ cups sugar

4 inches fresh ginger, peeled and sliced

2 teaspoons cream of tartar

1 tablespoon brewer's yeast

makes about 6 quarts

Cut the zest off the lemons in strips, then remove and discard the white pith. Thinly slice the lemon flesh, removing all the pits. Put the lemon flesh and zest in a large bowl and add the sugar, ginger, and cream of tartar. Add about 6 quarts boiling water and let stand until tepid.

Sprinkle in the yeast and stir. Cover with plastic wrap and let stand in a warm place for 24 hours. Using a large metal spoon, skim off the yeast, then carefully pour the mixture through a strainer, leaving behind any sediment. Pour into bottles with secure tops and leave for 2 days before drinking. Serve chilled with ice.

melon and strawberry juice

These summer fruits, now available all year round, make a delicious, refreshing drink. This is so quick to make, you can do so just before your guests arrive.

1 melon, such as cantaloupe or honeydew

2 cups strawberries, hulled

freshly squeezed juice of 2 limes

8 ice cubes, plus extra to serve

serves 4

Chop the melon flesh into small pieces and put in a blender. Add the strawberries, lime juice, and ice. Blend until smooth and serve in a large chilled pitcher.

Top tip: For a flavored yogurt drink, add some plain yogurt to the blender with the fruit.

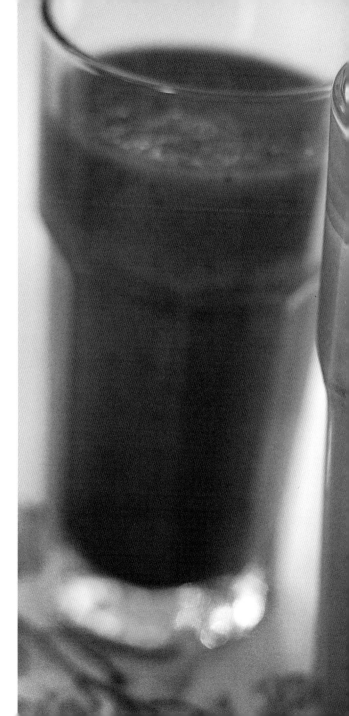

index

conversion charts

Weights and measures have been rounded up or down slightly to make measuring easier.

Volume equivalents:

American	Metric	Imperial
1 teaspoon	5 ml	
1 tablespoon	15 ml	
¼ cup	60 ml	2 fl.oz.
⅓ cup	75 ml	2½ fl.oz.
½ cup	125 ml	4 fl.oz.
⅔ cup	150 ml	5 fl.oz. (¼ pint)
¾ cup	175 ml	6 fl.oz.
1 cup	250 ml	8 fl.oz.

Weight equivalents:

Imperial	Metric
1 oz.	25 g
2 oz.	50 g
3 oz.	75 g
4 oz.	125 g
5 oz.	150 g
6 oz.	175 g
7 oz.	200 g
8 oz. (½ lb.)	250 g
9 oz.	275 g
10 oz.	300 g
11 oz.	325 g
12 oz.	375 g
13 oz.	400 g
14 oz.	425 g
15 oz.	475 g
16 oz. (1 lb.)	500 g
2 1b.	1 kg

Measurements:

Inches	Cm
¼ inch	5 mm
½ inch	1 cm
¾ inch	1.5 cm
1 inch	2.5 cm
2 inches	5 cm
3 inches	7 cm
4 inches	10 cm
5 inches	12 cm
6 inches	15 cm
7 inches	18 cm
8 inches	20 cm
9 inches	23 cm
10 inches	25 cm
11 inches	28 cm
12 inches	30 cm

Oven temperatures:

110°C	(225°F)	Gas ¼
120°C	(250°F)	Gas ½
140°C	(275°F)	Gas 1
150°C	(300°F)	Gas 2
160°C	(325°F)	Gas 3
180°C	(350°F)	Gas 4
190°C	(375°F)	Gas 5
200°C	(400°F)	Gas 6
220°C	(425°F)	Gas 7
230°C	(450°F)	Gas 8
240°C	(475°F)	Gas 9